Set design by Aaron P. Mastin

The set for the New York production of *Acts of Love*.

ACTS OF LOVE

BY KATHRYN CHETKOVICH

DRAMATISTS
PLAY SERVICE
INC.

ACTS OF LOVE
Copyright © 2009, Kathryn Chetkovich

All Rights Reserved

CAUTION: Professionals and amateurs are hereby warned that performance of ACTS OF LOVE is subject to payment of a royalty. It is fully protected under the copyright laws of the United States of America, and of all countries covered by the International Copyright Union (including the Dominion of Canada and the rest of the British Commonwealth), and of all countries covered by the Pan-American Copyright Convention, the Universal Copyright Convention, the Berne Convention, and of all countries with which the United States has reciprocal copyright relations. All rights, including without limitation professional/amateur stage rights, motion picture, recitation, lecturing, public reading, radio broadcasting, television, video or sound recording, all other forms of mechanical, electronic and digital reproduction, transmission and distribution, such as CD, DVD, the Internet, private and file-sharing networks, information storage and retrieval systems, photocopying, and the rights of translation into foreign languages are strictly reserved. Particular emphasis is placed upon the matter of readings, permission for which must be secured from the Author's agent in writing.

The English language stock and amateur stage performance rights in the United States, its territories, possessions and Canada for ACTS OF LOVE are controlled exclusively by DRAMATISTS PLAY SERVICE, INC., 440 Park Avenue South, New York, NY 10016. No professional or nonprofessional performance of the Play may be given without obtaining in advance the written permission of DRAMATISTS PLAY SERVICE, INC., and paying the requisite fee.

Inquiries concerning all other rights should be addressed to the Gersh Agency, 41 Madison Avenue, 33rd Floor, New York, NY 10010. Attn: Susan Cohen.

SPECIAL NOTE

Anyone receiving permission to produce ACTS OF LOVE is required to give credit to the Author as sole and exclusive Author of the Play on the title page of all programs distributed in connection with performances of the Play and in all instances in which the title of the Play appears for purposes of advertising, publicizing or otherwise exploiting the Play and/or a production thereof. The name of the Author must appear on a separate line, in which no other name appears, immediately beneath the title and in size of type equal to 50% of the size of the largest, most prominent letter used for the title of the Play. No person, firm or entity may receive credit larger or more prominent than that accorded the Author. The following acknowledgment must appear on the title page in all programs distributed in connection with performances of the Play:

Originally produced in New York City by
Dangerous Arrangement in November 2007.

ACTS OF LOVE was developed at the Harbor Theatre and produced by Dangerous Arrangement at the Kirk Theatre (later moving to the Lion Theatre) in New York City, opening on November 1, 2007. It was directed by Marc Geller; the set design was by Aaron P. Mastin; the costume design was by Dennis Ballard; the lighting design was by Frank DenDanto, III; the original music was by Daniel T. Denver; the original song, "September Man," was written and performed by Meg Flather; the production stage manager was Bernita Robinson; and the production assistant was Cristina Knutson. The cast was as follows:

ED	Andrew Dawson
SHEILA	Diane Tyler
TOM	Andrew Rein
ANNIE	Abby Royle

Understudy for SHEILA and ANNIE .... Tracey Gilbert

CHARACTERS

ED, 60
SHEILA, 49
TOM, 29
ANNIE, 29

PLACE

The living room of a summer cottage.

TIME

The present.

ACTS OF LOVE

Scene 1

Setting: simply furnished living room of a summer cottage by a lake. A front door is upstage; another door leads to the offstage kitchen and lake. Stairs upstage lead to offstage bedrooms. There is at least one window. Family photos — including, perhaps, a larger portrait of Tom's mother, Emily — are on a mantle or wall. Sheets cover the furniture.

At rise: Ed enters, carrying a suitcase and a large squash. He sets both down and wanders through the room, pulling off the sheets, opening windows, checking out the back porch — the homeowner inspecting his property. He picks up a pair of binoculars and begins looking out the window. Sheila enters, carrying a bag of groceries.

SHEILA. Smell that!
ED. What?
SHEILA. The air! Isn't that great? God.
ED. *(Taking a friendly but distracted sniff.)* Nice. That was quick. How'd you get away so fast?
SHEILA. I promised Marjorie we'd drop by later.
ED. *We?*
SHEILA. We don't have to stay long.
ED. What's wrong with people? Why can't they just leave a person alone?
SHEILA. It's known as neighborliness, Ed. Some people consider it a virtue.
ED. The same people who think an overgrown vegetable is an appropriate gift? *(Sheila takes groceries to the offstage kitchen, from*

which she can still be heard. Ed goes back to his binoculars.)
SHEILA. I'd forgotten what all was here. Canned peas. Clam chowder.
ED. *(Looking through binoculars.)* Another new house going up on the Pragers' lot. That man would rent out his tool shed if he could get somebody to live in it.
SHEILA. Water chestnuts and canned chow mein noodles!
ED. And the Rasmussens have taken down every tree that might have impeded a full view of their house from any direction. That's thoughtful. *(Sheila reenters.)*
SHEILA. Why is it that stuff you'd never think of eating at home tastes good when you're on vacation?
ED. Not thirteen-pound zucchinis. *(Sheila retrieves the squash, carries it to the kitchen, and returns.)*
SHEILA. It's like something out of a fairy tale — a cupboard full of free food!
ED. It's not free. You just don't remember paying for it.
SHEILA. It's like Daylight Savings Time. That extra hour.
ED. Standard Time.
SHEILA. Excuse me?
ED. That hour belongs to Standard Time.
SHEILA. You know what I mean.
ED. I'm just correcting you in the interest of accuracy.
SHEILA. Thank you.
ED. And of course that hour is no more free than those groceries. It's the same one we lose every spring.
SHEILA. But it feels like a gift by the time we get it back again.
ED. That's my point. It's not.
SHEILA. That's my point. It feels like it is.
ED. Well. It's not.
SHEILA. Is it really that important?
ED. Of course not. Rationality is only man's crowning achievement, what sets him apart from the rest of the rude beasts of creation. If you want to be part of the trend to take twenty-five hundred years of civilization back to its roots in superstition and magical thinking, be my guest.
SHEILA. Ed?
ED. What.
SHEILA. Is something the matter?
ED. What could possibly be the matter? *(Returning to the binocu-*

lars.) Good god, what's that monstrosity on the Ballards' deck? Some sort of medieval torture device? *(Sheila looks out the window.)*
SHEILA. It's a grill.
ED. It's obscene.
SHEILA. Then don't look.
ED. It's the size of Maryland! I can hardly ignore it. And you didn't mention the appalling color of Dan's new powerboat. *(Pause.)* When are they getting here?
SHEILA. Sometime this afternoon, he said.
ED. That means sometime tonight.
SHEILA. He's busy.
ED. How busy can he be? He's a cook!
SHEILA. *(Mocking him.)* It's not like he's a doctor, after all.
ED. *(Missing the mockery.)* Well, exactly. He avoids us.
SHEILA. He wants to celebrate our anniversary with us. That doesn't sound like avoiding to me.
ED. Nothing ever sounds as bad as it is to you. You think it's perfectly fine for him to waste his life scrambling eggs and frying hamburgers.
SHEILA. That's not what he does.
ED. Oh, so if it's tofu teriyaki and grilled-chicken wraps, that makes all the difference?
SHEILA. I honestly don't care what he does, so long as he's happy.
ED. Well, I do. And I'm not apologizing for that.
SHEILA. What a surprise.
ED. And what makes you so sure he's happy?
SHEILA. What makes you so sure he's not?
ED. If he were happy, he'd be doing something with his life!
SHEILA. You're being more horrible than usual.
ED. And I shudder to think what this girl will be like. God spare us from another model-activist.
SHEILA. Liberatoria! I liked her.
ED. You like them all. You liked that performance artist with the speech impediment, too.
SHEILA. That was *not* a speech impediment, that was some kind of … tongue jewelry. And she was very smart — that bit on Margaret Thatcher and Mother Teresa in the ladies' room was very clever.
ED. Margareth Thather and Mother Teretha.
SHEILA. You're just jealous.
ED. Of what? My own son and his apparently endless succession

of mutilated consorts? Don't be ridiculous. I just think it's time he got serious about someone and settled down.
SHEILA. It's precisely because he does take it seriously that he hasn't settled down.
ED. *Must* you look so relentlessly on the bright side of everything?
SHEILA. As opposed to your side, you mean?
ED. Doesn't he want a family?
SHEILA. He has plenty of time for that.
ED. Well, we don't.
SHEILA. You have to let him make his own choices, Ed.
ED. I don't see why parents have to pretend not to know better when they obviously do.
SHEILA. You don't know everything.
ED. I know a lot.
SHEILA. No point being modest about it, I guess.
ED. I'm just being honest. You remember honesty — it's one of those old-fashioned virtues that got dropped from the list to make room for neighborliness.
SHEILA. What about discretion? Did that get dropped too?
ED. He's my son. He has a right to know what I think.
SHEILA. Then let him ask. Please, Ed? Be nice this weekend?
ED. When am I ever —
SHEILA. Because I think Annie —
ED. That name! Can't you just hear her? "I, um, study art *history?* And it's really, like, *interesting?*"
SHEILA. Did it ever occur to you that if you really want Tom to settle down with one of these girls it might help if you were a little friendlier to them?
ED. You want me to ooh and aah over her tattoos?
SHEILA. I'm not asking for a miracle. Just try not to frighten her.
ED. You have obviously forgotten my capacity to charm.
SHEILA. It's not something people are supposed to have to *remember.*
ED. Is that a challenge? You'll see. By the end of the weekend I'll have her thinking, "I want this man to be the grandfather of my children."
SHEILA. Really, Ed. Simple cordiality will do.
ED. You really think I can't be nice? Am I that unlovable?
SHEILA. *(A little awkwardly.)* Of course not. I'm teasing you. *(She takes his hand.)* I'm glad we came.

ED. Happy anniversary, kid.
SHEILA. Happy anniversary.
ED. Come on. Let's take a walk down to the lake. *(They exit. Stage is empty for a moment before Tom and Annie enter.)*
TOM. *(Calling.)* Mom? Dad? Anybody home?
ANNIE. Oh, Tom, this is great! Smell that!
TOM. What?
ANNIE. The air! God, it's great.
TOM. *(With a sniff exactly like his father's.)* Nice.
ANNIE. If I were you, I'd come here all the time. It's like something out of a fairy tale or something.
TOM. One of those stories where the witch locks up the children and torments them with questions like "What are you going to do with your life?"
ANNIE. I wonder where they are.
TOM. Down at the lake, probably.
ANNIE. Should we go look?
TOM. Let's wait. This way, when things get tense, we can always suggest *going* to the lake. If we've already been to the lake, we don't have anywhere to go.
ANNIE. Planning your exit strategy already?
TOM. I can't remember the last time my father and I were in the same house for more than one meal. This is a five-meal visit.
ANNIE. *(Looking around.)* I love this place!
TOM. Including two dinners, one of which will be the obligatory celebration meal.
ANNIE. *(Picking up a framed picture.)* Is this you? You look adorable in a Stetson.
TOM. Why did I let you talk me into this?
ANNIE. It's their twentieth anniversary. You can't just send a card.
TOM. We could have met them for breakfast. Breakfast is a nice, *short* meal. That would have been perfect.
ANNIE. *(Back to the photos.)* Who's this next to you?
TOM. My brother.
ANNIE. I didn't know you had a brother.
TOM. I don't. He died. A long time ago. He drowned.
ANNIE. I'm sorry.
TOM. Don't be. It wasn't your fault.
ANNIE. I just mean —
TOM. It's OK. I know what you mean. Hey. Come here. *(He pulls*

her close. They kiss. Annie pulls away.) What's wrong?
ANNIE. Nothing. I just don't really want to be going at it when your parents walk in.
TOM. Don't worry — they're going to love you.
ANNIE. You really think so?
TOM. Of course! Just don't take anything my father says personally.
ANNIE. What about your mother?
TOM. No worries there. She always likes my girlfriends.
ANNIE. Oh.
TOM. I don't mean it that way.
ANNIE. I didn't think you did.
TOM. Actually, you might have heard of her. She's an anthropologist.
ANNIE. Really? Is her name Mackenzie?
TOM. Warren.
ANNIE. The only Warren I know of is Sheila Warren.
TOM. That's her.
ANNIE. Sheila Warren is your *mother?*
TOM. Stepmother, technically.
ANNIE. You're kidding, right?
TOM. Strange thing to joke about, don't you think?
ANNIE. Tom! Why didn't you tell me?
TOM. I didn't want you feeling like you had to — I don't know — prepare.
ANNIE. A pop quiz is better?
TOM. Don't worry about it. You don't have to impress her.
ANNIE. I know. No, I know.
TOM. You just have to impress me. *(Pause.)* I'm kidding. *(He pulls Annie close to kiss her again. She's still distracted, and jumps away from him at the sound of:)*
SHEILA. *(Offstage.)* Hellooo! *(Sheila and Ed enter through back door.)*
TOM. Mom! Dad! Hi!
ED. Tom! We didn't expect you this early.
TOM. If it's a problem —
SHEILA. Of course it's not a problem.
ED. Right. Just not what you told us, is all. But that's fine, of course! It's good to see you, son. And this must be —
TOM. Annie, I'd like you to meet my parents, Ed and Sheila.
ANNIE. *(Offering her hand.)* How do you do. I'm so glad to meet you. Both. It's an honor. A surprise, and an honor. *(Sheila stares at*

her for a moment, then looks at Tom, missing the offered hand. Ed takes her hand and shakes it.)

ED. We're delighted to meet you. Tom's told us all about you, of course.

ANNIE. He has?

SHEILA. Not very much, actually. Not nearly enough.

ED. Well, certainly not enough to do you justice, my dear — that much is obvious.

TOM. Dad? You OK?

ED. Couldn't be better!

TOM. Annie knows all about *you,* Mom.

SHEILA. She does? *(Forcing herself to look at Annie.)* You do?

ANNIE. From your work, of course. I'm a huge fan. But I had no idea until just a few minutes ago that you were Tom's mother. I was just telling him I wish he'd told me.

SHEILA. Surprises are always a bit awkward, aren't they?

TOM. Annie's studying anthropology. I think I might have mentioned that.

SHEILA. No, I don't think you did.

ED. Well, well. Another anthropologist in the family!

SHEILA. Ed.

ED. And isn't your mother looking well, Tom? Twenty years of marriage and she's still the most attractive woman I know.

SHEILA. Ed.

ED. Speaking of married life —

SHEILA. Ed!

ED. I just want to add that your mother and I are touched, and pleased, that you're here to help us celebrate our anniversary.

TOM. Well, good. That's great.

ED. *(To Sheila.)* Right, pet?

TOM. Pet?

SHEILA. Have you two brought your things in?

TOM. Not yet. I was thinking we might go down to the lake first.

ANNIE. Already?

ED. Excellent idea! Let's all go!

TOM. Weren't you just down there?

ED. Not with you!

SHEILA. Actually, there are a few things in the kitchen I should see to.

ANNIE. Can I help?

11

SHEILA. Maybe later.
ED. Why don't you two lovebirds head on down there, and I'll give Sheila a hand and join you in a minute.
TOM. Dad, are you really OK?
ED. Of course! Why do you ask?
TOM. I don't know, you just seem weirdly ... happy about everything.
ED. And why shouldn't I be? Smell that air!
TOM. Whatever you say. *(To Annie.)* Come on. Pet. *(Tom opens the back door.)* My god, that powerboat!
ED. Fabulous color, isn't it? *(Tom and Annie exit.)* Well! I think that went very well!
SHEILA. Shhh. Keep your voice down.
ED. I was really very welcoming, wasn't I?
SHEILA. You were fine.
ED. *You* were a bit cool, I thought.
SHEILA. Really, Ed, you're getting carried away with this whole thing. I wish you'd stop it.
ED. I think she might be The One.
SHEILA. For god's sake. You just met her.
ED. I've got a feeling about her.
SHEILA. Since when do you get feelings about people?
ED. She looks a lot like Emily, actually.
SHEILA. She does not.
ED. She does. The hair, for one thing. But also something about her eyes. Didn't you notice it?
SHEILA. No.
ED. You will. The resemblance is almost uncanny.
SHEILA. You better get going. They'll be wondering where you are.
ED. I'm right about this. You'll see. *(Ed exits. Finally alone, Sheila drops all pretense of routine and collapses on the couch. She's alone for a few moments. Annie enters, unnoticed at first. When Sheila finally sees her, she's startled.)*
ANNIE. Just me. Tom and ... Ed are still down at the lake. God, this is so —
SHEILA. What are you doing here?
ANNIE. I had no idea. I swear.
SHEILA. You expect me to believe that?
ANNIE. He never mentioned you.
SHEILA. And you didn't ask?

ANNIE. Why would I have asked?
SHEILA. You knew I had a son!
ANNIE. Am I supposed to ask every man I meet if he's your son?
SHEILA. I just don't see how this could have happened.
ANNIE. Maybe it's fate.
SHEILA. That's ridiculous.
ANNIE. Not to cultures all over the world.
SHEILA. Well, we're not all over the world. We're here.
ANNIE. I just think —
SHEILA. And since when is your name *Annie?*
ANNIE. That's what Tom calls me.
SHEILA. It's a cartoon name! I'm sorry. This is just such a shock.
ANNIE. For me, too!
SHEILA. Of course. I'm sorry.
ANNIE. It's so strange to see where you live.
SHEILA. We don't actually live here. It's just a summer place.
ANNIE. Still! Your furniture, your pictures — it's a little window into your life.
SHEILA. How are you? How have you been?
ANNIE. Fine! I'm fine! It's just — you know, strange to be here.
SHEILA. You look good. You look older.
ANNIE. I'm twenty-nine.
SHEILA. Right. *(Pause.)* Look, Ed doesn't know about you. I never told him.
ANNIE. I figured that. *(Pause.)*
SHEILA. So how did you meet — you and Tom?
ANNIE. At a party. You know Tom, he makes everything easy. He just came up and started talking. I liked him right away. Family resemblance, I guess.
SHEILA. That's impossible.
ANNIE. It happened.
SHEILA. The resemblance, I mean. He's not my son. Biologically.
ANNIE. Score another one for nurture over nature.
SHEILA. Is it serious between you two?
ANNIE. It might be.
SHEILA. Anne, I'm just not sure that's a good idea.
ANNIE. Maybe it's not up to you. *(Pause.)* Aren't you even a little bit glad to see me? *(Tom and Ed reenter.)*
ED. Miladies!
TOM. *Miladies?*

13

ED. What's the matter, a man can't use a little old-fashioned term of respect and endearment around here without everybody's eyebrows going up? Annie, you're on my side, aren't you?
ANNIE. Absolutely. I'm all for respect and endearment!
TOM. Annie? You OK?
ANNIE. Totally! A-OK! *(Pause.)* That lake is really something!
ED. Still somehow marvelous, despite every human effort to destroy it.
TOM. Says my father, who plans to take his motorboat out and go fishing tomorrow.
SHEILA. Would anyone like a glass of water? I was just — feeling thirsty. How about it? Tom? Ann-ie? Water?
ED. Oh, I'm sure we've got something more festive than water in there. This is an *occasion,* after all. It's not like we see you every week — or even every month.
TOM. OK, Dad. *(Sheila exits to kitchen.)*
ED. It's not like we see you every year, even.
TOM. *OK,* Dad.
ED. When *is* the last time we saw you? *(Tom almost responds, thinks better of it.)*
TOM. *(To Annie.)* So what did we interrupt?
ANNIE. Excuse me?
TOM. What were you two talking about?
ANNIE. Oh, nothing. Well, not nothing, obviously. Work. Your mother was telling me about her work.
TOM. You haven't been boring her, have you, Mom? *(Sheila enters with glasses of champagne on a tray. She hands them around.)*
SHEILA. Probably.
ANNIE. Champagne!
SHEILA. It was Ed's idea.
TOM. Nice choice, Dad.
SHEILA. We're so glad you're here, sweetheart. Both of you.
ED. Well! How about a toast?
TOM. To you two. Twenty years. That's an achievement.
ED. I think Sheila deserves most of the credit for that.
ANNIE. To Sheila, then!
ED. Hear, hear! *(They drink.)* So, my dear, tell us a little about yourself. How did you decide to study anthropology?
ANNIE. Well, I was a history major in college —
ED. Really! I always thought Tom had an aptitude for history, if

he'd only just applied himself.

TOM. I never had any interest in history, and you know it.

ED. Well you could have, if you'd applied yourself. That's all I'm saying.

TOM. *(To Annie.)* You see what I mean?

ANNIE. I'd love to hear how you two met.

SHEILA. Oh, we won't bore you with all that!

ANNIE. No, really. I'm curious.

ED. Ah, that reminds me! *(He heads across the room to the old stereo.)*

SHEILA. What?

TOM. Mom used to work at my father's clinic.

ED. Best receptionist I ever had.

SHEILA. I was not. I worked there all of six months while I was in grad school.

ED. It doesn't take long for excellence to show itself.

ANNIE. An office romance!

SHEILA. No, nothing like that. We didn't get together until much later.

TOM. My dad was already married back then.

SHEILA. That's right. To Emily, Tom's mother.

ANNIE. So what's your secret?

SHEILA. Sorry?

ANNIE. What's the secret to your long, obviously happy marriage?

SHEILA. Oh, I'm not sure we have one.

ANNIE. A happy marriage?

SHEILA. A secret.

ANNIE. Trust, maybe?

SHEILA. That's hardly a secret.

ED. I'll show you the real secret. *(By this point, Ed's placed a record on the turntable. The music begins: a jazzy ballad, perhaps.)*

SHEILA. Oh god, Ed. Where did you find this?

ED. *(Holding his arms out to Sheila.)* I happen to be a phenomenally good dancer.

SHEILA. Please, Ed. Not now.

ED. How about you, then, Annie? Will you indulge an old man?

ANNIE. I'd be happy to — but I don't really know how.

ED. Nothing to it, if you've got the right partner. *(He takes Annie in his arms.)* Just relax and follow me. *(As they take a few steps:)* I always told Tom every man should know three things: how to

work, how to defend himself …
TOM. And how to dance.
ED. But he wouldn't listen. Would you look at this girl? She's a natural! *(Lights down as they dance.)*

Scene 2

Later that afternoon. Tom standing on a wooden (or plastic) stepladder, working on a ceiling light fixture. Ed handing him tools.

TOM. There are three of them up here. Which one is it?
ED. The ground wire.
TOM. That's the white one, right?
ED. No, that's the neutral wire.
TOM. I thought the neutral wire *was* grounded.
ED. The ground wire, not the grounded wire. This is ridiculous. Let me get up there and do it.
TOM. I'll do it. If you would just tell me which one's the damned grounded wire!
ED. Not grounded, *ground.* I'll do it. You come down and hold the ladder.
TOM. Fine. Fine! *(Tom comes down the ladder. Ed takes his place. Sheila enters.)*
SHEILA. What are you doing up there? Tom, I told you —
TOM. He insisted.
SHEILA. Ed, get down from there. I'm not kidding.
ED. It's perfectly safe. I've done this a million times.
SHEILA. Why can't you let Tom do it?
ED. We tried that already.
SHEILA. What difference does it make, anyway? We never even use that light.
ED. It's broken. I know how to fix it, I'm going to fix it. Tom, hold the ladder steady.
SHEILA. I can't watch this. Where's Anne — Annie?
TOM. Down at the lake.

SHEILA. Why aren't you down there with her?
ED. Here it is, right here. The ground wire. I don't see what all the difficulty was.
SHEILA. Ed, I really don't like to see you on that ladder!
ED. Then don't look.
TOM. Everything's fine, Mom. *(Sheila exits.)*
ED. Your mother thinks it looks serious between you two.
TOM. I hate that word, *serious.* It's like, OK, the fun's over, now the work begins.
ED. The work has to begin sometime.
TOM. I know you think so.
ED. Hand me those wire cutters, would you? You know, you really ought to learn how to do this kind of thing. Comes in handy and it's really very satisfying, being able to do a few things around the house. Economical, too. You know what an electrician would charge for a little job like this? We had one come out to the clinic last week and — *(The phone rings. Ed, startled by the sound, begins to lose his balance.)* Oh! Whoa!
TOM. Dad! *(Ed slips and falls from the ladder. Tom grabs him.)* Got you. You OK?
ED. Yes, it's just my ankle, damn it. I think I may have twisted it.
TOM. Here. Lean on me. *(Ed waves him off and takes a few steps.)*
ED. I'll be fine. *(Sheila enters.)*
SHEILA. What happened?
ED. Nothing happened! The phone startled me and I lost my balance.
SHEILA. It's Marjorie calling. Something's wrong with Dan.
ED. Choked on a gigantic bell pepper, probably.
SHEILA. She sounds upset, Ed. She needs to talk to you.
ED. We just got here! Can't they at least wait until tomorrow to have their medical emergency?
SHEILA. Ed.
ED. All right. I'm coming. *(He follows Sheila offstage. To Tom:)* Never mind that. We'll call somebody to do it. *(Tom picks up the wire cutters and climbs the ladder again. Stares at the wires.)*
TOM. Fuck! *(Annie enters.)*
ANNIE. What is it?
TOM. We're leaving.
ANNIE. What are you talking about? Why? What happened?
TOM. I told you, this always happens. He's impossible! And now, this … fucking … light!

ANNIE. Maybe I can help.
TOM. Don't worry about it.
ANNIE. No, come on. Let me try. What are you trying to do — just replace the socket?
TOM. Really. It doesn't matter.
ANNIE. Then let me try. *(Tom climbs down, exasperated. Annie takes the wire cutters from him and heads up.)*
TOM. Be careful — it's dangerous if you don't know what you're doing.
ANNIE. *(Assessing the situation.)* As long as you don't forget the ground wire —
TOM. You know about the ground wire?
ANNIE. It's not that big a mystery.
TOM. I love you!
ANNIE. I bet you say that to all the girls.
TOM. I don't usually mean it. *(Ed enters, still limping. Sheila follows him on.)*
ED. Tom! What's she doing up there?
TOM. She knows about the ground wire!
ED. You really ought to learn about these things yourself, son.
TOM. Everything OK? On the phone?
SHEILA. Dan collapsed. Probably just the heat, but your dad is going over there to have a look.
TOM. OK.
ED. Actually, I could use your help.
TOM. Really?
ED. I'm not sure I can put all my weight on this leg at the moment, and we may need to help him inside.
TOM. Sure. OK.
ED. *(To Annie.)* I'm sorry about this. We shouldn't be long.
ANNIE. Of course. It's fine. I hope everything's all right.
TOM. When you're done with this, maybe you can replumb the shower? *(Tom and Ed exit. Annie, still on the ladder, goes to work.)*
SHEILA. Just leave that.
ANNIE. I like doing it. Gives me something to occupy my hands. *(She works. Sheila waits.)* So you never called.
SHEILA. I know. I'm sorry.
ANNIE. I gave up waiting. Obviously.
SHEILA. I thought I would. Call. I wanted to.
ANNIE. Well, it's the thought that counts! *(Pause.)* You look great.

SHEILA. Please don't say that.

ANNIE. You look like hell, then. Is that better? *(She goes back to work on the wires.)* I was just thinking about the first time I saw you.

SHEILA. I'd really rather not talk about that.

ANNIE. It wasn't at the conference, you know. It was a year before that, when you came to campus to give a talk. I was sitting in the back of this packed auditorium, and the president or somebody introduced you, and you walked up to the podium and before you said a word, you did something. Do you remember what?

SHEILA. Anne. Please.

ANNIE. You took off your watch. That's the first thing I remember — you taking something off.

SHEILA. I wanted to keep track of the time.

ANNIE. And then you slipped that little microphone over your head and cinched it up like a noose, and we could all hear it slide up your silk blouse. Like that sound of the sea in a seashell. What a tease. *(Pause. She holds her hand out.)* Screwdriver. *(Sheila hands her the tool.)*

SHEILA. How did you learn how to do things like this?

ANNIE. My father taught me.

SHEILA. I've never understood the first thing about electricity.

ANNIE. Almost nobody really understands it. That's one of the things I like about it.

SHEILA. You're sure it's not dangerous, what you're doing?

ANNIE. The power's off.

SHEILA. Oh. *(A little embarrassed.)* Of course. Well, there you are. My ignorance is showing.

ANNIE. But if you flip that circuit, I'll show you something exciting.

SHEILA. That's OK.

ANNIE. Go ahead. I need the juice back on to check the connection anyway. *(She gestures toward the circuit box, mounted on the wall.)* Right over there. *(Reluctantly, Sheila goes over to it.)* There's really only one thing you need to know about electricity: It wants to move. The only way it can hurt you is if it can move through you. And the only way it can move through you is if you're touching something. Or someone. OK. Flip it.

SHEILA. Now?

ANNIE. Now. *(Sheila flips the switch. Annie hesitates a moment, then touches her screwdriver to the hot wire.)* See? Nothing. But if you were to touch me right now, the current would knock you across the room. *(They look at each other for what seems like the first*

time.) Isn't that amazing? All that energy just waiting for the right — *(Tom enters, in a rush.)*
SHEILA. Tom!
TOM. Dad thinks Dan should go to the hospital, and Marjorie's not in any shape to take him.
SHEILA. What's wrong with him?
TOM. I don't know. Maybe a stroke.
SHEILA. I'll be right there.
TOM. It's OK. I'm going to drive. I just wanted to let you know.
SHEILA. But you just got here. You don't want —
TOM. It's no problem. I don't mind.
SHEILA. But you two came all this way. And I can easily —
TOM. Mom, he *asked* me. I want to do it.
SHEILA. What about Annie? Maybe she'd like to go along?
ANNIE. It sounds like I'd just be in the way. I'm fine here — *(To Sheila.)* — if that's OK with you?
SHEILA. Of course. It's fine.
TOM. Great. Then I better go. See you later?
ANNIE. We'll be right here.
SHEILA. Bye, sweetheart. *(He exits. Quiet again. Here, or later, Annie comes down from ladder.)* You could have gone.
ANNIE. So could you.
SHEILA. You heard me. I tried.
ANNIE. You could have insisted.
SHEILA. His father asked for his help. I'm not going to take that away from him.
ANNIE. So. Here we are. *(Pause.)*
SHEILA. Anne. What happened between us. It was very … nice. But it wasn't real.
ANNIE. You can't say what's real for someone else. You're the one who taught me that.
SHEILA. I just mean —
ANNIE. I know what you mean. I'm not stupid.
SHEILA. Of course you're not.
ANNIE. Yes I am. I should have known you were just fooling around.
SHEILA. I wasn't.
ANNIE. You can't have it both ways, you know. Either it mattered or it didn't. *(Pause.)*
SHEILA. That night — the night I met you — I couldn't believe

what was happening. I thought, OK, you're on vacation from your life. Just this one night, and then tomorrow everything goes back to normal. But then tomorrow came and I didn't want to go back. I wanted to spend another day with you, and then another. I started thinking maybe it wasn't vacation, after all. That I'd made my choice and lived one life, and now I was getting a chance to live another one. That's what I thought when I told you I would call. I really thought I would.
ANNIE. Then why didn't you?
SHEILA. Because it was Sunday when I got home.
ANNIE. And what? You'd suddenly found religion?
SHEILA. On Sundays Ed makes dinner. He always lines up all the ingredients on the kitchen counter, very meticulously, and when I walked in and saw the potatoes and carrots lying there, all the little spice jars, I knew I couldn't do it. Because what was going to happen to this life while I went off to live the other one? I couldn't do it. But I couldn't not do it. So every day I'd let myself pick up the phone and dial your number.
ANNIE. I don't believe you.
SHEILA. Three-two-three, four-three-six, two-zero-four.
ANNIE. Nine.
SHEILA. I always hung up before the nine. For a while there I felt like my whole marriage was hanging by the thread of that one little number. *(Pause.)* And then one day, finally, I realized I'd gone the whole day without picking up the phone.
ANNIE. Do you want me to leave?
SHEILA. I want you not to have come.
ANNIE. So it is real. Between us.
SHEILA. I thought you were in love with Tom.
ANNIE. Not like this. *(Annie stands there, close but unmoving. Sheila looks at her, taking her in.)*
SHEILA. I still can't believe it. "Of all the gin joints in all the towns in all the world … "
ANNIE. I walked into yours.
SHEILA. It's almost like I conjured you.
ANNIE. All those phone calls. Maybe you did. You know that thing Jung said about meaningful coincidences.
SHEILA. I'm the one who told *you* what Jung said.
ANNIE. Well, I was listening. To everything you said. *(Pause.)* Maybe it is fate, Sheila.

SHEILA. I told you, I don't believe in that.
ANNIE. Maybe it doesn't matter what you believe. Maybe what matters is what you want. *(Sheila hesitates, begins to turn away, then turns back again. They kiss.)*

Scene 3

Later that night. Annie and Sheila playing Scrabble. Annie has just finished laying down her tiles.

SHEILA. "Dwergmal"?
ANNIE. It's a Norse word.
SHEILA. We're allowing Norse words?
ANNIE. You could challenge.
SHEILA. That's all right.
ANNIE. Want to know what it means?
SHEILA. Nobody likes a showoff.
ANNIE. Plus the triple-word score, that's like ninety points, right? *(Sheila calculates the score.)*
SHEILA. You won. Again.
ANNIE. This is why you should never play Scrabble with a grad student. We read all the time and we remember everything. Let's go upstairs.
SHEILA. Let's play again.
ANNIE. And if I win, we go upstairs. *(Sheila, about to shuffle the tiles for another game, stops. She stands and moves away from the couch.)* I read *your* book again recently. The first one.
SHEILA. Be nice. I had no idea how much the field was about to change when I wrote that book.
ANNIE. It's an amazing piece of work. That's why people still read it.
SHEILA. I said Be nice. I didn't say Lie.
ANNIE. I'm not. Somehow, within the context of a traditional ethnography, you managed to anticipate the critique of the asymmetrically othering discourses of an imperialist worldview. *(Pause.)* OK, I've been rehearsing that line for months.
SHEILA. *(Suddenly serious.)* What made you think you'd get a

chance to use it? *(Suddenly, the sounds of Ed and Tom's arrival — car doors slamming or just their voices outside the door — can be heard. The women fall silent, looking at each other. Ed and Tom enter.)*
ANNIE. Hi!
ED. What are you two still doing up?
ANNIE. Playing Scrabble!
TOM. *(To Sheila.)* I thought you hated Scrabble.
ANNIE. *(To Sheila.)* I told you we should have played something else.
SHEILA. *(To Ed.)* How is … everything? With Dan, I mean.
ED. He'll be fine. Anaphylactic shock. Imagine, being allergic to bees all these years and never knowing it! But Marjorie may have had a heart attack.
SHEILA. What?!
ED. Seeing Dan unconscious — it was quite a shock.
SHEILA. No!
ED. It happens.
ANNIE. God.
TOM. I know. Unbelievable, right?
SHEILA. Where is she?
ED. They admitted her. They'll know more in the morning.
SHEILA. Where's Dan?
ED. He's still there. I told him there's nothing he can do for her, he might as well come home and get a good night's sleep in his own bed, but he wouldn't leave her.
TOM. What time is it, anyway?
ED. *(Checking his watch.)* Good god, it's after midnight.
SHEILA. Well. It's been a long day. We should all probably turn in.
ANNIE. I'm not very sleepy.
TOM. Neither am I.
SHEILA. You two stay up then. Just — do what you like.
ED. *(To Annie.)* I'm sorry. This isn't turning out to be much of a weekend, I'm afraid.
ANNIE. I'm having a wonderful time. Really.
ED. At least you two had a chance to get acquainted.
ANNIE. We did.
ED. And I think I might be able to guess at least one topic of conversation.
TOM. Not now, OK, Dad?
ED. I know I'm not supposed to mention it, but I can't resist: Congratulations!

ANNIE. Excuse me?
TOM. Dad. Didn't we just — ?
ED. I'm sorry, Tom — but I can't keep that kind of news from your mother.
SHEILA. What news?
ED. Well, go on, son! Cat's out of the bag now! *(Without giving him a chance to speak; to Sheila:)* They're getting married! What did I tell you?
ANNIE. Tom!
TOM. Dad!
ANNIE. Why did you tell him that?
TOM. I shouldn't have, I know.
ED. *(To Annie.)* Don't be too angry with him, dear. It's hard not to share good news. *(To Sheila.)* And this is very good news, isn't it?
SHEILA. It's — a little hard to believe.
ED. I'm surprised Annie didn't tell you herself.
SHEILA. I guess she's just better at keeping a secret.
ED. And imagine: all this from a chance meeting in a restaurant! It's kismet!
SHEILA. What restaurant?
TOM. My restaurant, Mom. Obviously.
SHEILA. *(To Annie.)* I thought you said you met at a party.
ANNIE. We did.
TOM. That's where we really *talked* for the first time. But we met when Annie and her friend came in for dinner.
SHEILA. That's remarkable.
TOM. What's remarkable about it?
SHEILA. Just that of all the gin joints in all the world …
TOM. People do go there, Mom.
SHEILA. I know that, sweetheart. But Dad's right. It seems almost fated, doesn't it?
ANNIE. I thought you didn't believe in fate.
ED. Sometimes there's just no better explanation!
SHEILA. And that you would have spoken to each other! *(To Tom.)* You don't usually leave the kitchen, do you?
TOM. *(To Annie.)* Can I tell her?
ANNIE. It's really not that interesting.
SHEILA. Oh, I'm sure it is.
ED. She sent a note to the chef, complimenting the meal.
ANNIE. Tom!

TOM. *(To Annie.)* Don't be embarrassed. My dad loved hearing that.

SHEILA. What an extraordinary thing to do.

ANNIE. We really liked the food.

SHEILA. Apparently!

TOM. *(To his mother.)* Is that so hard to believe?

SHEILA. Of course not. You're a wonderful cook. But people don't often send love notes to the chef in your restaurant, do they?

ANNIE. It wasn't a love note.

TOM. It was pretty friendly. You invited me to a party!

ANNIE. That was after you came out to meet us.

TOM. Well, you certainly got my attention.

ED. Good for you! Tom needs an assertive woman!

SHEILA. *(To Annie.)* By the way, what did you have?

ANNIE. Excuse me?

SHEILA. What did you have to eat that made such an impression?

ANNIE. Some kind of pasta, I think.

SHEILA. So you don't actually remember.

TOM. It was a primavera.

ANNIE. That's right. Anyway, my friend and I were the last people in the restaurant that night, and she thought it would be fun to meet the cook.

SHEILA. That's odd. I've never once been in a restaurant and thought that.

TOM. Of course not.

ANNIE. Well, my friend did.

SHEILA. And yet you were the one who wrote the note. Right?

TOM. She set her little trap and I walked right into it.

ANNIE. I did not!

TOM. Am I complaining? I loved it!

SHEILA. And you were the one who invited him to the party?

ANNIE. That was actually my friend's idea, too.

SHEILA. I'd love to meet your friend sometime. Maybe at the wedding.

ED. This young woman obviously knows what she wants. I admire that!

SHEILA. *(To Annie.)* So it wasn't a complete coincidence, was it? Your meeting?

TOM. How is it a coincidence at all?

SHEILA. It's not.

ANNIE. It doesn't have to be a coincidence to be the right thing, does it? What matters it that we're here. What matters is how we feel.
ED. Exactly right! And we're delighted you're here and it's all worked out so well.
SHEILA. Yes. And now it really is getting late. Come on, Ed. Let's give these two a little privacy. I'm sure they'd like a little time alone together.
TOM. Thanks, Mom.
ANNIE. Yes. Thank you. For having us here.
SHEILA. You're welcome. You're always welcome. You and Tom.
ED. *(To Annie.)* Good night, my dear. You've made us very happy. *(He kisses her on the forehead. He turns to Tom. Pats his shoulder.)*
TOM. Good night, Dad. Good night, Mom. *(Tom kisses his mother.)*
SHEILA. Good night, sweetheart. *(Sheila and Annie hesitate for a moment, then hug good night.)*
ANNIE. See you in the morning, then?
SHEILA. You bet. *(Sheila and Ed exit up the stairs.)*
TOM. Before you start: I know. I'm sorry.
ANNIE. What the hell is going on?
TOM. I don't know. When I saw that woman — her heart stopping because she thought her husband was going to die? That's love, Annie! That's what we're in this for!
ANNIE. To fall down dead of a heart attack?
TOM. For someone to mean everything to you. For your own life to be so wrapped up with someone else's that you can't imagine living without them!
ANNIE. You don't just *decide* to feel that way about someone, Tom.
TOM. I'm sick of just drifting. I want to settle down and make something with somebody.
ANNIE. Even if what you're making is a big mistake?
TOM. Yes! I'm ready to make some big mistakes! I want to make some big mistakes with you!
ANNIE. Oh, Tom. Why did you have to tell him that?
TOM. I don't know. I could just feel him looking at my aimless, pointless, unfocused life —
ANNIE. He said that?
TOM. Not exactly.
ANNIE. Then how do you know that's what he was thinking?
TOM. Because it's what he's always thinking! So will you?

ANNIE. What?

TOM. Marry me.

ANNIE. So you can get your father's approval? No!

TOM. Forget my father. I love you.

ANNIE. Tom, we've never even talked about this before!

TOM. OK, fine, we're talking about it now! The subject is officially on the table! Do you want to, or not?

ANNIE. Not if that's the way you ask!

TOM. I'm sorry. Let me try that again.

ANNIE. Look, Tom, I've been thinking, too. And I just don't think —

TOM. That's the problem! Too much thinking!

ANNIE. No. I don't think that is the problem.

TOM. See? More thinking! OK. Look. Let's not get all — Let's just —

ANNIE. Tom —

TOM. I know — wait. Just — just wait. *(He walks over to the stereo and drops the needle. Music starts to play, very softly.)*

ANNIE. We need to —

TOM. Do this. We need to do this. *(He pulls her to him.)*

ANNIE. I thought you didn't know how to dance.

TOM. I know how to sway.

ANNIE. I'm really pretty tired.

TOM. So sleep. *(He puts her head on his shoulder. They sway.)* My dad asked me tonight if I wanted this place.

ANNIE. The house?

TOM. We were on our way back here. I was driving, and after a while he fell asleep. It felt like one of those moments when suddenly everything turns around, you know? Like I was the father and he was the kid. It was so peaceful and lonely, just listening to him breathe and driving in the dark. And when he woke up, he asked me if I wanted the house.

ANNIE. Was this before or after you told him we were getting married?

TOM. I don't remember. It was all part of the same conversation.

ANNIE. It sounds like a bribe. Get married, settle down, and I'll give you the house.

TOM. But the thing is, I could see it too. I could see you and me spending summers here. Maybe even living here, who knows? *(Annie breaks away from him, and walks over to the stereo. The music stops.)* Does it sound like such a bad life?

ANNIE. Tom, I need to tell you something. *(Pause.)* Sheila and I got to talking tonight. About all sorts of things.

TOM. She likes you, I can tell.

ANNIE. I like her, too. A lot.

TOM. I knew you would. That's why I didn't tell you about her before.

ANNIE. Because you knew I'd like her?

TOM. Because I wanted to make sure it was me you loved and not my famous mother.

ANNIE. Oh, Tom —

TOM. I know, it was stupid.

ANNIE. No, it wasn't. It wasn't. *(Pause.)* You know, it turns out I met her once. Last year. She came to campus for this conference —

TOM. See? That's what I mean! It's like, everything is finally starting to come together. Like this is what's supposed to happen. You know what my father said tonight that really got to me? It wasn't about the house or getting married or any of that. He told me all the things he remembered about the day I was born. You know how many times we've talked about that day before? Never. It felt so fucking … *normal.*

ANNIE. You *are* normal, Tom. You're a wonderful, normal person.

TOM. Is that a criticism?

ANNIE. No! God, no. I'm just not sure we're right for each other.

TOM. Because you're so abnormal, you mean?

ANNIE. Not abnormal. Just … different.

TOM. You don't think I'm different?

ANNIE. Of course I do. I don't even know what we're talking about!

TOM. You think I'm simple because I want to get married and try to be happy.

ANNIE. I do *not* think that.

TOM. People think happiness is such a superficial thing to want. But if you don't have it, it's everything. Jesus. Look at my mother.

ANNIE. You don't think your mother's happy?

TOM. Not Sheila. My real mother. She was so unhappy it killed her.

ANNIE. What are you talking about? I thought she died in a car accident.

TOM. She did. A one-car accident on a bright, sunny day. Drove right into a tree.

ANNIE. Still, that doesn't mean —
TOM. Six weeks after my brother died. *(Pause.)* She'd already pretty much given up sleeping and eating at that point, so it was sort of the next logical step.
ANNIE. Oh, god. Tom. I'm sorry.
TOM. You know, I sometimes think about the day he died — how if it had rained that day, we wouldn't have gone swimming, and everything would have been different. Something else might have happened, but it wouldn't have been that.
ANNIE. You can't think that way.
TOM. Oh yes you can.
ANNIE. I wish you'd told me this before. *(She embraces him.)*
TOM. Now you'll have to marry me. Out of pity. *(He begins to kiss her.)*

Scene 4

Early the next morning. Tom is sitting on the couch, holding a piece of paper. Sheila enters, walking down the stairs.

SHEILA. Good morning, sweetheart.
TOM. Morning.
SHEILA. You're up early.
TOM. I'm not the only one.
SHEILA. Pardon?
TOM. You're up early, too.
SHEILA. Right. I suppose I am. *(Pause.)*
ED. *(Coming down the stairs.)* Morning, all!
TOM. Morning, Dad.
ED. Stunning day! You know, Tom, I was just thinking — your mother and I talked at one point about knocking out a wall in the master bedroom and putting in a picture window. I bet Annie would love that.
TOM. I don't think so.
ED. Of course she would. Women love windows. I'll ask her myself when she comes down.

SHEILA. How about some breakfast?
ED. Great idea. We haven't had a proper meal since you two got here! *(Phone rings. Sheila steps into the kitchen to answer it.)*
SHEILA. *(On phone.)* Hello? ... Oh, hello, Dan. ... Not at all, we were just talking about you. How's Marjorie? ... Oh, good. That's great, great news. ... Yes, he's right here. Hold on. *(Ed is shaking his head and backing away.)* Actually, Dan, he just stepped into the shower, but I'll be sure to tell him ... Oh, you don't need to do that. A cab will cost you a fortune. I'd be happy to come get you ... No problem at all. *(She hangs up.)* Marjorie's been released. She's fine, apparently.
ED. And now you're offering to pick them up? No shortage of neighborly virtue in this house!
SHEILA. It won't take long. You could have talked to him.
ED. I could tell from your end that everything was fine.
SHEILA. He might have liked to tell you that himself!
ED. That's what I was afraid of.
SHEILA. Honestly, Ed! The man could have died yesterday!
ED. And I saved his life! Isn't that enough? Am I now supposed to spend an hour on the phone hearing how grateful he is?
SHEILA. Sometimes I don't understand you at all. How you can be so —
TOM. Annie's gone.
SHEILA. What?
ED. Will she be back in time for breakfast?
TOM. She's not coming back.
ED. What?
TOM. She left me this. I found it when I woke up. *(He holds up the piece of paper.)*
SHEILA. What is that?
TOM. A note!
ED. Why would she leave you a note? What does it say?
TOM. Just — things.
ED. If this has anything to do with what we talked about last night —
TOM. It doesn't. So can we just forget it?
ED. You could let me finish my sentence!
TOM. I don't want the house, Dad. OK?
ED. But if you and Annie are getting —
TOM. We're not! We're not getting married.

ED. I thought it was all settled.
TOM. Well, it's not.
ED. That's ridiculous! What did you do?
TOM. Nothing.
ED. You must have done *something*. You must have *said* something.
TOM. Why do you assume it's all my fault?
ED. Because it usually is!
TOM. Well, it isn't this time.
ED. You've got to start taking some responsibility in your life, Tom!
SHEILA. Ed.
TOM. Would you listen to me, Dad? For just one second? Annie doesn't want to marry me, and there's nothing I can do about it! OK?
ED. You can't just expect everything to fall into your lap, son. You have to *work* at things.
TOM. She doesn't love me!
ED. Of course she does!
TOM. No she doesn't. She loves someone else.
ED. Well, *who,* for pete's sake?
SHEILA. Ed, let him be.
ED. And that's it? You're giving up, just like that? Women don't expect you to take news like that lying down. When are you going to learn to go after what you want?
TOM. Like you did, you mean?
ED. What?
TOM. Like you did. With my mother.
ED. I don't know what you're referring to.
TOM. She got to be such a bummer, but you didn't let that stop you, right? You went ahead and got what you wanted.
ED. That was a very different situation. The circumstances were entirely —
TOM. That's right. She made it easy on you by killing herself.
ED. That is completely uncalled for.
TOM. But true.
ED. Your mother's death was an accident.
TOM. Oh, Dad! Come on!
ED. She was very ill. You know that.
TOM. So why didn't you help her?
ED. I'm not going to dignify that with a response.
TOM. That's convenient.
ED. What are you implying?

TOM. Just that things worked out the way you wanted in the end, didn't they? The defective model replaced by a much more satisfactory one.
ED. I won't stand for you insulting her!
TOM. I'm not insulting her! I'm insulting you!
SHEILA. Stop it! Both of you! Stop it!
TOM. Never mind. I don't care. She was obviously crazy —
SHEILA. She wasn't!
TOM. Locking herself in her room all day? Burning all of her clothes? Is that what healthy, happy people do?
SHEILA. She was distraught.
TOM. That was always the word, wasn't it? Like she was some character from a nineteenth-century novel.
SHEILA. You can't know what it was like for her.
TOM. Oh, right. The depth of her misery, the agony of losing a child and blah blah blah.
SHEILA. Don't talk that way.
TOM. It doesn't matter.
SHEILA. Yes it does! Stop saying that! It all matters!
TOM. Let's just forget it.
SHEILA. She loved you! She loved you and your brother more than anyone on this earth.
TOM. Loved us to death, I guess you could say! *(Sheila slaps him, hard.)*
SHEILA. Oh, my god. I'm sorry, Tom. *(Tom turns to walk away.)*
ED. Come back here and apologize to your mother!
SHEILA. No. Don't.
ED. Tom! I'm speaking to you! *(Tom keeps walking toward the door.)* Do you have any idea how much she was looking forward to this visit? I'm not about to let you just walk out and ruin it!
TOM. I'd say it's pretty well ruined already, wouldn't you?
ED. You're making a big mistake here.
TOM. For once in your fucking life, would you please please not say that! *(He exits.)*
SHEILA. Ed —
ED. Don't defend him.
SHEILA. It's not his fault.
ED. You can't be forever stepping in to protect him. This is precisely what happens when you do!
SHEILA. What is?

ED. You saw him! He storms off instead of facing things! He blames someone else! He's got to develop some backbone!
SHEILA. He has a right to feel hurt.
ED. Over something that happened more than twenty years ago?
SHEILA. Over something that happened last night!
ED. You know how it is with young people. They're always breaking up. It's recreational. *(He sees the note, still on the couch, and takes a step toward it. Sheila sees what he's doing and grabs the letter first. He stares at her.)* Why did you do that?
SHEILA. It's Tom's. It doesn't belong to you.
ED. It doesn't belong to you, either. *(Pause.)*
SHEILA. I met her once. Anne. Annie.
ED. I fail to see what that has to do with anything, frankly.
SHEILA. We spent some time together.
ED. So you remembered her? Why didn't you say so?
SHEILA. I didn't want you to know.
ED. Why on earth not? *(Pause.)*
SHEILA. It was at that conference last fall. The college always sends a grad student to meet you at the airport, and she was the one who picked me up. It was the night of that huge storm, remember?
ED. Vaguely.
SHEILA. My flight was already late, and then the traffic was horrendous, so by the time we finally got to the hotel, we'd already missed the dinner. So we just went to a coffee shop to get something to eat, and we ended up talking. For hours.
ED. Sounds tedious.
SHEILA. It wasn't. *(Pause.)* I spent the night with her. *(Pause.)*
ED. What are you saying?
SHEILA. She came back to my room. We spent the night together.
ED. Are you telling me you slept with that girl?!
SHEILA. Yes. *(Pause.)* It was just that one weekend. I never spoke to her again. I thought I would never see her again.
ED. Then why did you let her come here? To our home!
SHEILA. I had no idea she was coming.
ED. But you didn't send her away. You didn't tell her to leave.
SHEILA. She was Tom's guest.
ED. And you didn't want to be rude? Is that it?
SHEILA. I thought if she and Tom really loved each other …
ED. We'd find a way to work it out. Just one big, happy family.
SHEILA. In time, yes. Maybe.

ED. You were willing to try. For Tom's sake.
SHEILA. Yes.
ED. That's awfully noble of you. *(Pause.)* But she wasn't here because she really loved Tom, was she?
SHEILA. Apparently not.
ED. You must have asked her.
SHEILA. What?
ED. What she was doing here.
SHEILA. I did. She said it was all a big coincidence, that she had no idea I was Tom's mother, that they'd met at a party and he'd never mentioned anything —
ED. Did she ever once say she was in love with him?
SHEILA. No.
ED. Then you didn't let her stay for Tom's sake, did you? You let her stay for yours. *(Pause.)* Are you in love with her?
SHEILA. I hardly know her.
ED. That's a comfort. *(Pause.)* Were you ever going to tell me?
SHEILA. No.
ED. You didn't think it was any of my business?
SHEILA. I didn't think you'd understand.
ED. So you decided to make sure I understood by not telling me.
SHEILA. I thought it would hurt you.
ED. No more than being lied to.
SHEILA. I'm sorry, then. It was a mistake not to tell you.
ED. Well, it's all on the table now.
SHEILA. Yeah.
ED. Then tell me why you did it.
SHEILA. I don't know.
ED. That's not good enough.
SHEILA. It was such a strange night. We'd spent all these hours together, talking, and suddenly something else was happening. I can't explain it, it was just …
ED. Just one of those things? One of those crazy bells that now and then rings? *(Pause.)* Was that it? *(No answer.)* Sheila? Was that it?
SHEILA. Yes.
ED. You better go.
SHEILA. What do you mean?
ED. Dan and Marjorie are waiting for you.
SHEILA. Oh, god. I completely forgot. I'll ask Tom —
ED. No. You go.

SHEILA. I'd rather stay here. With you.
ED. No.
SHEILA. Ed — *(He walks away from her. Sheila follows him.)* Ed, please.
ED. No! Please just ... go. *(Sheila hesitates, then goes for her purse and leaves. Ed takes a few steps around the room and then begins to break down. He falls to his knees, crying. Tom enters.)*
TOM. Dad? *(Ed gets up, keeping his face averted.)* Dad!
ED. I thought you said you were leaving.
TOM. I am.
ED. So leave already.
TOM. I'll need a ride.
ED. Ask your mother.
TOM. Where is she?
ED. Gone.
TOM. Do you know when she'll be back?
ED. No.
TOM. Dad? What's the matter?
ED. I don't know. I don't know a fucking thing!
TOM. OK. *(Pause. Unsure what to do, Tom reaches out but is unable to actually touch his father. He begins to back off toward the stairs.)* I'll just — be upstairs.
ED. I did try to help her, you know. Your mother.
TOM. Maybe we should talk about it later.
ED. You don't believe me. *(Pause.)* There was nothing I could do. There was nothing anybody could do. She became unreachable. You were too young to remember, but —
TOM. I remember.
ED. It was as if she'd already died. She'd be sitting there at the table in that horrible unwashed robe, refusing to eat, refusing to speak —
TOM. Maybe if you'd paid more attention to her! Maybe if you hadn't fallen in love with someone else!
ED. Is that what you think happened?
TOM. How naive do you think I am? Mom dies, and suddenly Sheila's around all the time? And, like, a year later, you're married?
ED. It was two years.
TOM. Whatever.
ED. Listen to me: I never betrayed your mother. Never.
TOM. You just didn't save her.
ED. You'd like it to be all my fault, wouldn't you?

TOM. I just want you to admit that some of it was! She was my mother!

ED. I lost her, too, you know. And I lost my son.

TOM. I know that. God! Do you think I'm not aware of that every fucking day? The son you could have had?

ED. What are you talking about?

TOM. I'm talking about the fact that everything about my life disappoints you!

ED. That is just not true.

TOM. Don't you think I want you to be proud of me? The one son you have left? Don't you think I want you to be glad that *I'm* alive?

ED. Where do you get these ideas? That's the most idiotic —

TOM. You know what? Forget it. Just forget it. *(He turns to leave.)*

ED. Is this your idea of talking? Say whatever you want and then walk away?

TOM. Is this your idea of it? Calling me an idiot?

ED. I would never —

TOM. You just did.

ED. You know what I meant.

TOM. Why do I always have to know what you mean? Why can't you ever just say it?

ED. I haven't been a very good father. I know that! But that has absolutely nothing to do with how much I love you. *(Suddenly, unexpectedly, they embrace. And break off again, with their customary awkwardness.)*

TOM. You had breakfast yet?

ED. I'm not hungry.

TOM. Yes, you are. You just don't know it. *(Tom takes a step toward the kitchen, turns to wait for his father. Ed hesitates, then joins him. They exit together. Lights dim.)*

Scene 5

Two hours later. Ed, lying on the couch. Sheila enters. He doesn't move or look over.

SHEILA. Hi.
ED. Hello.
SHEILA. What are you doing?
ED. Lying on the couch. I would have thought that was obvious. *(She walks over to him.)*
SHEILA. Dan and Marjorie can't stop singing your praises.
ED. That's nice.
SHEILA. They're just sort of clinging to each other. It's touching.
ED. They'll get over it. *(Pause.)*
SHEILA. I drove by the Robinsons'. They put in a hot tub, of all things. *(Pause.)* With a little mermaid statue.
ED. Sounds lovely. *(Sheila picks up the binoculars and holds them out to him.)*
SHEILA. You can probably see it from here. *(Ed looks at her but makes no move for the binoculars.)* She reminded me of Emily. *(Pause.)* I loved her, Ed.
ED. I thought you hardly knew her.
SHEILA. Emily. *(Pause.)* I was in love with Emily.
ED. You had an affair with her. You had an affair with my wife.
SHEILA. I've wanted to tell you that for a long time.
ED. Well. Now you have. *(Pause.)* Anyone else?
SHEILA. Excuse me?
ED. Anyone else I should know about? Did you sleep with anyone else?
SHEILA. No!
ED. That's it, then? My wife and my son's girlfriend.
SHEILA. Yes. *(He stands and begins to walk toward the stairs.)* Don't you want to talk about it?
ED. I don't think so. Not today. Not on our anniversary.
SHEILA. It was all over between us long before you and I ever —
ED. It was over because she died!

SHEILA. It was over before then.
ED. Not by much.
SHEILA. What?
ED. You were still seeing each other that spring, weren't you?
SHEILA. How did you know that?
ED. I asked her.
SHEILA. And she told you.
ED. She was my wife.
SHEILA. So you knew all this time. And you never said anything.
ED. *I* never said anything?
SHEILA. I promised her I wouldn't.
ED. What about your promise to me? *(Pause.)* The promise of our life together. The promise to love each other above all others.
SHEILA. I *have* loved you!
ED. Not above all others.
SHEILA. Ed, that was so long ago. I hardly even remember who I was then.
ED. I remember who you were. I remember the way I used to stand in my office, just inside the door, so I could listen to you talk to the patients in the waiting room. Just listening to your voice. And knowing you were the person I wanted to be with, the person I was *meant* to be with — but I already had a life, and a family, with someone else, and it wasn't going to happen. *(Pause.)* Tom was right: This life with you is the one I wanted all along.
SHEILA. You can't know how you would have felt if —
ED. Yes I can. This is what I always wanted. Just the way you always wanted her.
SHEILA. I wanted this, too.
ED. Not always.
SHEILA. No. Not always. But for a long time. *(Nothing happens for a long moment. Finally, Ed walks away, leaving the room. Sheila, left alone, walks over to the stereo and puts on the record. She stands there as the music begins, waiting. After a moment, Ed reappears. They look at each other. He crosses the room, picks up the binoculars, and looks out the window.)*
ED. You didn't mention the ghastly blue tile. *(Pause.)* And it looks as though that mermaid statue is actually a fountain.
SHEILA. I thought it might be.
ED. And I see they're repaving the driveway — the better to make room for all their hot-tubbing friends in their oversized recreational

vehicles, no doubt.
SHEILA. Maybe it won't be as bad as that.
ED. Worse. I promise you. It will be worse. *(Blackout.)*

End of Play

PROPERTY LIST

Sheet (covering furniture)
Couch
Large zucchini
Suitcase(s)
Bag of groceries
Binoculars
Framed family photos (little boys)
Bottle of champagne
4 glasses
Old record player and records
Wooden or plastic stepladder
Hand tools (screwdriver, wire cutters)
Medical bag
Lighting fixture with exposed wires
Fuse box (mounted on wall)
Scrabble game
Scorepad and pencil
Piece of paper (Annie's note)
Sheila's purse (or just set of car keys)

SOUND EFFECTS

Song playing on record player
Phone ringing

NEW PLAYS

★ **GUARDIANS by Peter Morris.** In this unflinching look at war, a disgraced American soldier discloses the truth about Abu Ghraib prison, and a clever English journalist reveals how he faked a similar story for the London tabloids. "Compelling, sympathetic and powerful." –*NY Times.* "Sends you into a state of moral turbulence." –*Sunday Times (UK).* "Nothing short of remarkable." –*Village Voice.* [1M, 1W] ISBN: 978-0-8222-2177-7

★ **BLUE DOOR by Tanya Barfield.** Three generations of men (all played by one actor), from slavery through Black Power, challenge Lewis, a tenured professor of mathematics, to embark on a journey combining past and present. "A teasing flare for words." –*Village Voice.* "Unfailingly thought-provoking." –*LA Times.* "The play moves with the speed and logic of a dream." –*Seattle Weekly.* [2M] ISBN: 978-0-8222-2209-5

★ **THE INTELLIGENT DESIGN OF JENNY CHOW by Rolin Jones.** This irreverent "techno-comedy" chronicles one brilliant woman's quest to determine her heritage and face her fears with the help of her astounding creation called Jenny Chow. "Boldly imagined." –*NY Times.* "Fantastical and funny." –*Variety.* "Harvests many laughs and finally a few tears." –*LA Times.* [3M, 3W] ISBN: 978-0-8222-2071-8

★ **SOUVENIR by Stephen Temperley.** Florence Foster Jenkins, a wealthy society eccentric, suffers under the delusion that she is a great coloratura soprano—when in fact the opposite is true. "Hilarious and deeply touching. Incredibly moving and breathtaking." –*NY Daily News.* "A sweet love letter of a play." –*NY Times.* "Wildly funny. Completely charming." –*Star-Ledger.* [1M, 1W] ISBN: 978-0-8222-2157-9

★ **ICE GLEN by Joan Ackermann.** In this touching period comedy, a beautiful poetess dwells in idyllic obscurity on a Berkshire estate with a band of unlikely cohorts. "A beautifully written story of nature and change." –*Talkin' Broadway.* "A lovely play which will leave you with a lot to think about." –*CurtainUp.* "Funny, moving and witty." –*Metroland (Boston).* [4M, 3W] ISBN: 978-0-8222-2175-3

★ **THE LAST DAYS OF JUDAS ISCARIOT by Stephen Adly Guirgis.** Set in a time-bending, darkly comic world between heaven and hell, this play reexamines the plight and fate of the New Testament's most infamous sinner. "An unforced eloquence that finds the poetry in lowdown street talk." –*NY Times.* "A real jaw-dropper." –*Variety.* "An extraordinary play." –*Guardian (UK).* [10M, 5W] ISBN: 978-0-8222-2082-4

DRAMATISTS PLAY SERVICE, INC.
440 Park Avenue South, New York, NY 10016 212-683-8960 Fax 212-213-1539
postmaster@dramatists.com www.dramatists.com

NEW PLAYS

★ **THE GREAT AMERICAN TRAILER PARK MUSICAL music and lyrics by David Nehls, book by Betsy Kelso.** Pippi, a stripper on the run, has just moved into Armadillo Acres, wreaking havoc among the tenants of Florida's most exclusive trailer park. "Adultery, strippers, murderous ex-boyfriends, Costco and the Ice Capades. Undeniable fun." –*NY Post.* "Joyful and unashamedly vulgar." –*The New Yorker.* "Sparkles with treasure." –*New York Sun.* [2M, 5W] ISBN: 978-0-8222-2137-1

★ **MATCH by Stephen Belber.** When a young Seattle couple meet a prominent New York choreographer, they are led on a fraught journey that will change their lives forever. "Uproariously funny, deeply moving, enthralling theatre." –*NY Daily News.* "Prolific laughs and ear-to-ear smiles." –*NY Magazine.* [2M, 1W] ISBN: 978-0-8222-2020-6

★ **MR. MARMALADE by Noah Haidle.** Four-year-old Lucy's imaginary friend, Mr. Marmalade, doesn't have much time for her—not to mention he has a cocaine addiction and a penchant for pornography. "Alternately hilarious and heartbreaking." –*The New Yorker.* "A mature and accomplished play." –*LA Times.* "Scathingly observant comedy." –*Miami Herald.* [4M, 2W] ISBN: 978-0-8222-2142-5

★ **MOONLIGHT AND MAGNOLIAS by Ron Hutchinson.** Three men cloister themselves as they work tirelessly to reshape a screenplay that's just not working—*Gone with the Wind.* "Consumers of vintage Hollywood insider stories will eat up Hutchinson's diverting conjecture." –*Variety.* "A lot of fun." –*NY Post.* "A Hollywood dream-factory farce." –*Chicago Sun-Times.* [3M, 1W] ISBN: 978-0-8222-2084-8

★ **THE LEARNED LADIES OF PARK AVENUE by David Grimm, translated and freely adapted from Molière's *Les Femmes Savantes*.** Dicky wants to marry Betty, but her mother's plan is for Betty to wed a most pompous man. "A brave, brainy and barmy revision." –*Hartford Courant.* "A rare but welcome bird in contemporary theatre." –*New Haven Register.* "Roll over Cole Porter." –*Boston Globe.* [5M, 5W] ISBN: 978-0-8222-2135-7

★ **REGRETS ONLY by Paul Rudnick.** A sparkling comedy of Manhattan manners that explores the latest topics in marriage, friendships and squandered riches. "One of the funniest quip-meisters on the planet." –*NY Times.* "Precious moments of hilarity. Devastatingly accurate political and social satire." –*BackStage.* "Great fun." –*CurtainUp.* [3M, 3W] ISBN: 978-0-8222-2223-1

DRAMATISTS PLAY SERVICE, INC.
440 Park Avenue South, New York, NY 10016 212-683-8960 Fax 212-213-1539
postmaster@dramatists.com   www.dramatists.com

NEW PLAYS

★ **AFTER ASHLEY by Gina Gionfriddo.** A teenager is unwillingly thrust into the national spotlight when a family tragedy becomes talk-show fodder. "A work that virtually any audience would find accessible." –*NY Times*. "Deft characterization and caustic humor." –*NY Sun*. "A smart satirical drama." –*Variety*. [4M, 2W] ISBN: 978-0-8222-2099-2

★ **THE RUBY SUNRISE by Rinne Groff.** Twenty-five years after Ruby struggles to realize her dream of inventing the first television, her daughter faces similar battles of faith as she works to get Ruby's story told on network TV. "Measured and intelligent, optimistic yet clear-eyed." –*NY Magazine*. "Maintains an exciting sense of ingenuity." –*Village Voice*. "Sinuous theatrical flair." –*Broadway.com*. [3M, 4W] ISBN: 978-0-8222-2140-1

★ **MY NAME IS RACHEL CORRIE taken from the writings of Rachel Corrie, edited by Alan Rickman and Katharine Viner.** This solo piece tells the story of Rachel Corrie who was killed in Gaza by an Israeli bulldozer set to demolish a Palestinian home. "Heartbreaking urgency. An invigoratingly detailed portrait of a passionate idealist." –*NY Times*. "Deeply authentically human." –*USA Today*. "A stunning dramatization." –*CurtainUp*. [1W] ISBN: 978-0-8222-2222-4

★ **ALMOST, MAINE by John Cariani.** This charming midwinter night's dream of a play turns romantic clichés on their ear as it chronicles the painfully hilarious amorous adventures (and misadventures) of residents of a remote northern town that doesn't quite exist. "A whimsical approach to the joys and perils of romance." –*NY Times*. "Sweet, poignant and witty." –*NY Daily News*. "Aims for the heart by way of the funny bone." –*Star-Ledger*. [2M, 2W] ISBN: 978-0-8222-2156-2

★ **Mitch Albom's TUESDAYS WITH MORRIE by Jeffrey Hatcher and Mitch Albom, based on the book by Mitch Albom.** The true story of Brandeis University professor Morrie Schwartz and his relationship with his student Mitch Albom. "A touching, life-affirming, deeply emotional drama." –*NY Daily News*. "You'll laugh. You'll cry." –*Variety*. "Moving and powerful." –*NY Post*. [2M] ISBN: 978-0-8222-2188-3

★ **DOG SEES GOD: CONFESSIONS OF A TEENAGE BLOCKHEAD by Bert V. Royal.** An abused pianist and a pyromaniac ex-girlfriend contribute to the teen-angst of America's most hapless kid. "A welcome antidote to the notion that the *Peanuts* gang provides merely American cuteness." –*NY Times*. "Hysterically funny." –*NY Post*. "The *Peanuts* kids have finally come out of their shells." –*Time Out*. [4M, 4W] ISBN: 978-0-8222-2152-4

DRAMATISTS PLAY SERVICE, INC.
440 Park Avenue South, New York, NY 10016 212-683-8960 Fax 212-213-1539
postmaster@dramatists.com www.dramatists.com

NEW PLAYS

★ **RABBIT HOLE by David Lindsay-Abaire.** Winner of the 2007 Pulitzer Prize. Becca and Howie Corbett have everything a couple could want until a life-shattering accident turns their world upside down. "An intensely emotional examination of grief, laced with wit." –*Variety.* "A transcendent and deeply affecting new play." –*Entertainment Weekly.* "Painstakingly beautiful." –*BackStage.* [2M, 3W] ISBN: 978-0-8222-2154-8

★ **DOUBT, A Parable by John Patrick Shanley.** Winner of the 2005 Pulitzer Prize and Tony Award. Sister Aloysius, a Bronx school principal, takes matters into her own hands when she suspects the young Father Flynn of improper relations with one of the male students. "All the elements come invigoratingly together like clockwork." –*Variety.* "Passionate, exquisite, important, engrossing." –*NY Newsday.* [1M, 3W] ISBN: 978-0-8222-2219-4

★ **THE PILLOWMAN by Martin McDonagh.** In an unnamed totalitarian state, an author of horrific children's stories discovers that someone has been making his stories come true. "A blindingly bright black comedy." –*NY Times.* "McDonagh's least forgiving, bravest play." –*Variety.* "Thoroughly startling and genuinely intimidating." –*Chicago Tribune.* [4M, 5 bit parts (2M, 1W, 1 boy, 1 girl)] ISBN: 978-0-8222-2100-5

★ **GREY GARDENS book by Doug Wright, music by Scott Frankel, lyrics by Michael Korie.** The hilarious and heartbreaking story of Big Edie and Little Edie Bouvier Beale, the eccentric aunt and cousin of Jacqueline Kennedy Onassis, once bright names on the social register who became East Hampton's most notorious recluses. "An experience no passionate theatergoer should miss." –*NY Times.* "A unique and unmissable musical." –*Rolling Stone.* [4M, 3W, 2 girls] ISBN: 978-0-8222-2181-4

★ **THE LITTLE DOG LAUGHED by Douglas Carter Beane.** Mitchell Green could make it big as the hot new leading man in Hollywood if Diane, his agent, could just keep him in the closet. "Devastatingly funny." –*NY Times.* "An out-and-out delight." –*NY Daily News.* "Full of wit and wisdom." –*NY Post.* [2M, 2W] ISBN: 978-0-8222-2226-2

★ **SHINING CITY by Conor McPherson.** A guilt-ridden man reaches out to a therapist after seeing the ghost of his recently deceased wife. "Haunting, inspired and glorious." –*NY Times.* "Simply breathtaking and astonishing." –*Time Out.* "A thoughtful, artful, absorbing new drama." –*Star-Ledger.* [3M, 1W] ISBN: 978-0-8222-2187-6

DRAMATISTS PLAY SERVICE, INC.
440 Park Avenue South, New York, NY 10016 212-683-8960 Fax 212-213-1539
postmaster@dramatists.com   www.dramatists.com